This Book Belongs To:

_ _

_ _

_ _

" Happy Easter, my little bunny "

♥ MAKE THE READING SPACE COZY AND INTERESTING.

- **Lighting:**
  To avoid putting undue strain on the baby's growing eyes, use gentle, natural lighting or stay away from too bright artificial lighting.

- **Positioning:**
  The baby's ideal visual range at this age is 8 to 12 inches from their face, so you might consider positioning the book accordingly.

- **Timing:**
  Consider choosing quiet, conscious times when your baby seems most open to interaction, such as after a meal or nap

- **Add Sounds:**
  Include straightforward, captivating noises that complement the picture. Say "beep beep" for an automobile or "baa baa" for a sheep, for instance.

- **Signs of Engagement:**
  Look for coos, movements, or prolonged focus as signs the baby is enjoying the activity.

♥ CONSIDER INCORPORATING THE BOOK INTO KEY MOMENTS OF YOUR BABY'S DAY

- **Tummy Time:**
  Hold the book up during tummy time to help strengthen your baby's neck muscles and encourage visual focus.

- **Bedtime Routine:**
  Make it part of your bedtime ritual to create a calming association with books and bonding

- **On The Go:**
  Use the book for extra stimulation by reading it during quiet moments in a car seat or stroller.

- **Signs of Overstimulation:**
  If the baby looks away, fusses, or closes their eyes, take a break and try again later.

RABBIT

Hop-hop! Rabbits are quick and love carrots.

BEAR

Look! A little bear is cozy inside the egg, ready to share a hug with you

FLOWER

A little flower blooms, just like our love.>

egg

A cute egg, full of surprises, just like you

BUNNY

Look! The Easter bunny is hopping to bring you some love

Basket

A cute egg, full of surprises, just like you

CHICK

Cheep, cheep! A little chick is saying hello to you

CARROT

Yummy, a crunchy carrot for the bunny to nibble on

LAMB

The Easter lamb is soft and cuddly, just like you

RAINBOW

A rainbow after the rain, bringing you joy and colors

EGG HUNT

Let's go on an egg hunt, where every egg is full of giggles

DUCK

Quack-quack! Ducks love splashing in the water.

DEER

Graceful and quiet, the deer walks in the forest.

COFFEE CUP

Daddy loves his coffee, and you're his sunshine!

SNAIL

Slow and steady, the snail carries its home.

FISH

Swish, swish! The little fish swims all day.

FROG

Ribbit-ribbit! Frogs love to leap in the pond.

TURTLE

With a hard shell, the turtle takes its time.

GiRL

This is a girl. She is happy

LLAMA

Hello, llama! You're fluffy and full of charm.

CAT

Purr-purr, the cat is napping on a sunny spot.

PANDA

So soft and cuddly, pandas love bamboo snacks.

CROCODILE

Snap! Watch out for the crocodile's big teeth.

FOX

Sneaky and clever, the fox says hello!

DOG

Woof! Let's wag our tails like a happy dog.

ELEPHANT

Trumpet like an elephant with a long, long trunk!

WHALE

Splish-splash! This big whale swims deep in the ocean.

HEDGEHOG

A little hedgehog rolls up tight-so cozy!

KANGAROO

Boing, boing! Let's hop like a kangaroo!

koala

Hold on tight like a koala climbing a tree.

BEAR

Big and cuddly, this bear gives the best hugs!

LiON

Roar! Can you roar like the king of the jungle?

I hope you and your little one are enjoying the magical journey of bonding through our book, crafted with love to nurture your baby's earliest moments. Each page is designed with care, bringing high-contrast drawings and heartfelt words to life for your newborn's

Your thoughts mean the world to me. If this book has brought a smile to your baby's face or created cherished moments in your family, I would be deeply honored if you could share your review. A few kind words from you can inspire other parents to create similar beautiful experiences with their little ones.

Your feedback isn't just valuable—it's a guiding light for me. If there's anything I could improve, or if you have suggestions to make My books even more special, please don't hesitate to reach out. Your voice helps me grow, learn, and serve families like yours better every day.

Together, let's make every parent-child moment extraordinary. Thank you for taking the time to write your review and for being part of this wonderful journey with me.

ztitacat@gmail.com

COPYRIGHT © 2025

---

ztitacat

This book, or any part of it, cannot be copied or shared in any form without written permission from the publisher, except for short quotes used in reviews.

We'd love to hear your thoughts!
If you enjoyed our book, please consider leaving us positive feedback on Amazon.
Your support means so much to us!